anythink

WAY TO GROW! GARDENING

FLOWERS

by Rebecca Pettiford

Ideas for Parents and Teachers

Pogo Books let children practice reading informational text while introducing them to nonfiction features such as headings, labels, sidebars, maps, and diagrams, as well as a table of contents, glossary, and index.

Carefully leveled text with a strong photo match offers early fluent readers the support they need to succeed.

Before Reading

- "Walk" through the book and point out the various nonfiction features. Ask the student what purpose each feature serves.
- Look at the glossary together. Read and discuss the words.

Read the Book

- Have the child read the book independently.
- Invite him or her to list questions that arise from reading.

After Reading

- Discuss the child's questions. Talk about how he or she might find answers to those questions.
- Prompt the child to think more. Ask: What is your favorite flower? Have you ever grown flowers yourself?

Pogo Books are published by Jump!
5357 Penn Avenue South
Minneapolis, MN 55419
www.jumplibrary.com

Library of Congress Cataloging-in-Publication Data

Pettiford, Rebecca, author.
 Flowers / by Rebecca Pettiford.
   pages cm. – (Way to grow! Gardening)
 Includes index.
 ISBN 978-1-62031-231-5 (hardcover: alk. paper) –
 ISBN 978-1-62496-318-6 (ebook)
 1. Flower gardening–Juvenile literature. 2. Flowers–Juvenile literature. I. Title. II. Series: Pettiford, Rebecca. Way to grow! Gardening.
 SB406.5.P485 2015
 635.9–dc23

                                         2015000276

Series Editor: Jenny Fretland VanVoorst
Series Designer: Anna Peterson
Photo Researcher: Anna Peterson

Photo Credits: All photos by Shutterstock except: Getty, 16–17, 18–19; iStock, 12–13; SuperStock, 6–7; Thinkstock, 1, 10–11, 14, 23.

Printed in the United States of America at Corporate Graphics in North Mankato, Minnesota.

TABLE OF CONTENTS

CHAPTER 1

COLOR YOUR GARDEN

Flowers add color to a garden. They smell good, too!

What flowers do you like?

Tulips in spring?
Sunflowers in summer?
Marigolds in fall?

You have many choices.
Where do you start?

First, decide what you want to plant. Some flowers need sun. Others need shade.

Find a space in your garden where your flowers will get the light they need.

DID YOU KNOW?

Many insects and birds like flowers. If you want to see butterflies, plant aster and goldenrod. Hummingbirds like petunia and zinnia.

sunflowers

CHAPTER 2

TYPES OF FLOWERS

Some flowers can be bought in pots and replanted. Others you can grow yourself from seeds or **bulbs**.

◀······ bulb

You plant **annuals** every year.
They last for one growing season.

Annuals include zinnia
and many sunflowers.

zinnia

Some flowers are **perennials**. They will flower for many growing seasons.

Lilies and tulips are perennials. They grow from bulbs.

DID YOU KNOW?

Do you have a favorite color? Yellow? Red? Or maybe you like them all.

You can choose what flowers to plant based on color. Here are some ideas:

RED = Cosmos, Zinnia

ORANGE = Dahlia, Marigold

YELLOW = Daffodil, Sunflower

GREEN = Bells of Ireland, Sweet Annie

PURPLE = Aster, Statice

WHITE = Shasta Daisy, Stock

lilies

daffodils

Plant **hardy bulbs** in the fall. These bulbs need cold weather to grow in the spring.

Plant **tender bulbs** in the spring and watch them flower in summer.

DID YOU KNOW?

Dig up tender bulbs in the fall. Store them in a dry place like a basement for the winter. Then plant them again in the spring!

CHAPTER 3

PLANTING FLOWERS

Are you ready to plant?

Use a small shovel to dig up the ground. Turn the soil over with a garden rake.

Smooth it out. You want your garden soil to be loose. This makes it easier for the roots to spread out.

You will need to dig holes for seeds, bulbs, or flowers that are in pots. Put them in the holes. Add **compost** to the soil. Use a small rake to fill in any extra space with dirt.

Then lightly water your plants. You can use a watering can or garden hose.

Use **mulch** to fill in around your flowers. It helps hold in moisture and keeps weeds from taking root.

Remember to water your flowers regularly. And don't forget to weed!

DID YOU KNOW?

Herbs are plants used in cooking or medicine. Some herbs have their own pretty flowers and can add more color to your garden.

mulch

When your flowers **bloom**, you can cut them and bring them inside. Put them in a vase so you can enjoy them.

Next spring is a new growing season. What flowers will you plant?

DID YOU KNOW?

Many flowers will bloom a second time if you pick off dead flower heads. This is called deadheading.

ACTIVITIES & TOOLS

TRY THIS!

PAPER POT SEED STARTERS

Give your flowers a head start and plant their seeds inside in early spring. You can make your own pots out of old newspaper.

What You Need:
- newspaper
- soil
- 5.5-ounce (156-gram) juice can
- flower seeds

1 Rip newspaper into three-inch-wide (8-centimeter-wide) strips.

2 Take a newspaper strip and roll it around the juice can, leaving about 1.5 inches (4 cm) of newspaper hanging over the bottom.

3 Fold the extra newspaper against the bottom of the juice can to create a flat, solid bottom.

4 Turn the can upright and press down firmly.

5 Remove the juice can. You have made a newspaper pot!

6 Fill each pot with soil. Stop a half an inch (1.3 cm) from the top. Plant your seeds following packet instructions.

GLOSSARY

annuals: Plants that last for one growing season.

bloom: When a plant blooms, its flowers open up.

bulbs: Plants that grow from an underground mass of tissue.

compost: A rotted mix of leaves, grass, and paper that makes garden soil healthy.

hardy bulbs: Bulbs that you plant in the fall; they need cold weather to grow in spring.

mulch: Dead leaves or wood chips that you spread around a plant; mulch helps control weeds and keep the soil moist.

perennials: Plants that grow for many seasons after the first time you plant them.

tender bulbs: Bulbs that you plant after the weather is warmer, usually in spring.

INDEX

TO LEARN MORE

Learning more is as easy as 1, 2, 3.

1) Go to www.factsurfer.com

2) Enter "flowers" into the search box.

3) Click the "Surf" to see a list of websites.

With factsurfer, finding more information is just a click away.